'Know the Game' Series

SHOT GUN SHOOTING

D0726772

CONTENTS

don'ts, both legal and moral. True sportsmen observe them, some regrettably less than others.

You will find much good advice in this excellent book which is primarily for the beginner to help him learn how to shoot accurately and safely so that he kills cleanly and does not harm his fellow-men.

Remember at all times that the future of game shooting is in your hands. If you take care to preserve game by shooting sensibly, you will increase your sport. Do the reverse and you will have only yourself to blame for lack of it.

The dwindling countryside is part of our heritage, to be preserved and handed on to succeeding generations, and this applies equally whether you live in an urban or a rural area. Only by acting with responsibility will you and those who come after you be able to continue to enjoy happy days with friendly company in some of the finest surroundings the country can produce.

FOREWORD

This new edition of Know the Game – Shot Gun Shooting is full of facts and figures which will be of interest to the beginner as well as to the person who thinks he knows it all.

Long before gunpowder was invented, man used to hunt with slings and bows and arrows, and there were few "regulations" to observe. Today it is a pastime in which hundreds of thousands take part, spending millions of pounds annually, with a thousand and one do's and

Chairman
Shooting Committee
British Field Sports Society

THE GUN

To the uninitiated, the general classification of shotguns may appear to be complicated but the following simple explanations will help you to understand some of the finer points.

A shotgun barrel is smooth inside whereas a rifle barrel is grooved along its length in a gentle spiral. Barrels come in various diameters; the term "bore" being used with a number to denote the nominal diameter 8, 10, 12 16, 20 and 28 bore guns are in common use nowadays, the higher the number, the smaller the diameter of the bore. The numbering originated in the early days of gunmaking and was based on the number of spherical balls of solid lead fitting the gun bore which together would weigh 1 lb. For example, 12 lead balls of 0.729″ diameter weigh 1 lb, therefore a 12 bore gun has a nominal diameter of 0.729″.

There are three guns which are exceptions to this method, being designated by their bore diameters; these are the Fourten (.410), and the 9mm and .22″ Garden guns.

Which bore gun you choose depends on the type of shooting to be done, but the 12 bore is probably the best for all normal use in this country, from wildfowling to game and rough shooting. The 16 bore, with slightly less range than the 12 bore, is also a popular choice, and the standard weapon in some parts of the world.

Smaller bore guns are usually much lighter and therefore guns such as the 20 and 28 bores are often used by ladies or young people. The Fourten and Garden guns are ideal for pest destruction.

GUN TYPES

The "Hammer Gun" (fig. 2) is now generally considered a thing of the past although there are still a few manufactured mainly on the Continent. They are generally very reliable but have a very distinct disadvantage compared with the "Hammerless Gun" (fig. 3) in that they have no "safe" catch. When early hammer guns of the non-rebounding type are being loaded, the hammer should be pulled back into the "half-cock", where they are normally quite safe to be carried about as they cannot normally be fired from this position. When shooting is in progress, the hammers are pulled back to the full-bent or full-cock position, but (and here is the danger) if the gun is not fired then, to be safe, the hammers must be lowered: this can only be achieved by taking the tension off the hammer with the thumb, pulling the trigger and gently lowering the hammer. The danger in doing this is obvious.

Fig. 2. A "hammer" gun

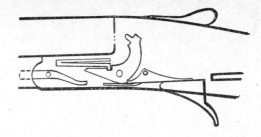

4(a). Cocked and ready to fire

4(b). After pressing trigger

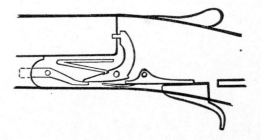

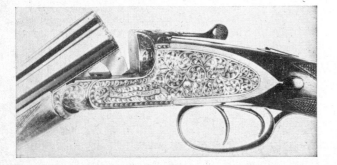

Fig. 3. A "hammerless" gun

Fig. 4. Firing pin mechanism of a boxlock "hammerless" gun

4

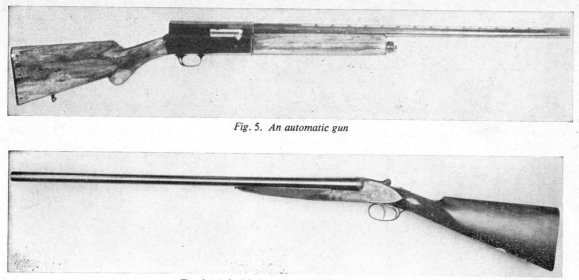

Fig. 5. An automatic gun

Fig. 6. A double-barrelled side lock ejector gun

There are five types of gun in general use today. These are:—

(a) Single barrel, which may be of the break open or bolt-operated type.

(b) Side by side double barrel, which may be of either sidelock or boxlock type.

(c) Over and under double barrel, which may also be of sidelock or boxlock type.

(d) Pump, which is a single barrel gun with a magazine (generally tubular under the barrel) from which cartridges are fed by the shooter 'pumping' the fore-end back and forward.

(e) Automatic, which is also a single barrel gun with a magazine, but the cartridges are fed in by the recoiling action of the gun which is operated by the explosion of the first cartridge.
(Some autos are not recoil-operated.)

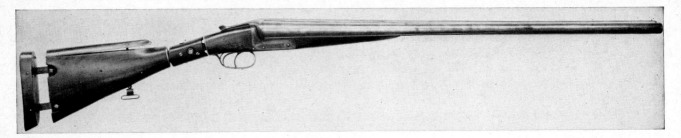

Fig. 7. Try gun

In the hammerless guns, the tumblers that strike the firing pin are internal and are cocked by the opening of the gun. The safety on these guns is often automatic, which means that when the gun is opened and therefore cocked, cartridges may be quite safely inserted and the gun closed and carried about, as the safe will automatically be "on", and must be pushed off by the thumb before the gun can be fired. If a gun has no automatic safe then the safety should be always pushed on to the safe position before opening the gun to reload. The safety should always be pushed to safe position if the shot is not taken.

Double barrel hammerless guns of type (b) and (c) may be of the boxlock type, i.e. with the working parts enclosed in slots machined in the body, or of the sidelock type, i.e. with the working parts fixed on detachable plates which in turn are let into the side of the body. The sidelock type is usually the better quality gun and generally costs a great deal more than the boxlock type.

CHOKE

Shot gun barrels usually have a certain degree of "choke" – that is a slight reduction of the diameter of the bore at the muzzle end. The greater the amount of choke, the closer the pellets in the shot charge will group together (i.e. form a pattern) at a given range.

In the normal double barrel guns used for game shooting, the right barrel is generally fired first and operated by the front trigger. The choke in this barrel is usually bored to improved cylinder; while that of the left barrel to $\frac{1}{2}$ or $\frac{3}{4}$ choke. This may be varied for different kinds of shooting. Single barrel guns of all types may be fitted with a variable choke, which is a device by which the amount of choking can be altered simply by turning a knurled ring on the muzzle end of the barrel.

A "true cylinder" boring means that there is no constriction of choke and this will give a 40% pattern in a 30″ circle at 40 yards. "Improved cylinder" will give a 50% pattern, and "Full choke" a 70% pattern.

GUN FITTING

Speed in mounting the gun and firing the shot is the essential part of using a shotgun and as we are not all the same shape and size nor have the same eyesight, it is

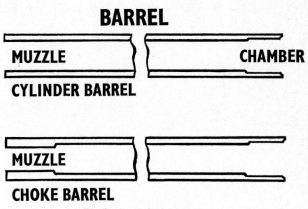

Fig. 8. A – Cylinder barrel
B – Choke barrel

necessary for the gun to "fit" perfectly. To enable the gunmaker to ensure this he has a "try-gun" (fig. 7) which has a stock adjustable in all directions. Combining the use of the "try-gun" with his fitting experience, the gunmaker will ensure that the gun is mounted by the shooter correctly every time. If he has to "pull" the gun on to the target then the fitting is incorrect.

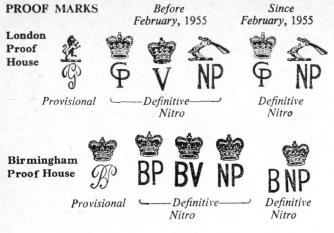

Fig. 9. Proof marks

PROOF MARKS

The Gun Barrel Proof Acts of 1868 and 1950 require that all guns, whether new or secondhand, must be proved and bear valid proof marks before they may be sold. The Acts impose penalties for selling, offering for sale, or other disposal of unproved arms, or arms which have been unduly reduced in substance or strength since they were last proved. It should be noticed that a gun once validly proved does not necessarily remain so indefinitely. The mere presence of proof marks does not establish that the barrels are "in Proof" for they may have been altered or weakened by boring out to remove pitting and the Proof Marks thereby rendered invalid.

When a gun is proved, it is tested to ensure that it is properly constructed and that it has a safe margin of strength to withstand, in normal use, the pressures developed by the cartridge for which it is chambered. A new gun of British manufacture will have been tested before it is offered for sale. Secondhand guns offered for sale by gunmakers may be expected to have a sound margin of safety, but if a secondhand gun is bought from an acquaintance, a secondhand dealer, or someone not *au fait* with Proof Regulations it is wise to have it checked by a gunmaker before completing the purchase. He will be able to advise as to its condition and, if the action or barrels of the gun have been altered, the gunmaker will know whether it should be submitted to a reproof or further test.

Double barrel shotguns receive two proofs during the course of their manufacture, a provisional proof and a definitive proof. Barrels only are submitted to provisional proof in the tube state to establish their soundness so that the gunmaker does not waste time and money making up defective material into a finished gun. Definitive proof is a test of the barrel and action when the gun is almost complete. These tests have been carried out at the London Proof House since 1637 and at the Birmingham Proof House since 1813. Guns so proved will be found to bear on the flats of the barrels near the breech, one or other of the proof markings in fig. 9.

Other marks are used to indicate the bore of the gun, the chamber length, the nominal bore diameter and the maximum service load, or since 1955, the maximum service pressure for which the gun has been proved.

Under the latest Rules of Proof, introduced in February, 1955, the view mark, that is the 'V' of the London Proof House and the 'BV' of the Birmingham Proof House, was discontinued and the new mark 'BNP' surmounted by a crown was introduced at Birmingham to replace the earlier 'BP' and 'NP'. The new proof Regulations do not affect the validity of earlier proof markings.

Some guns of foreign manufacture proved in this country will be found to bear encircled proof marks – this distinction between British proof markings on British and Foreign arms was in use only between 1925 and 1955.

Guns of foreign manufacture bearing the proper proof marks of Austria, Belgium, Czechoslovakia, France, West Germany, Italy and Spain are accepted in this country as proved arms and do not require to be submitted to British proof. All other guns of foreign manufacture not bearing acceptable proof marks must be submitted to proof in this country before they may be offered for sale. But care should be taken in presuming the validity of proof marks on old guns bearing Austrian, Italian and German proof marks used prior to 1939 and during the second World War, for those marks are not now valid in this country. Proof in France was optional until July, 1960, and some French guns bear marks which appear to be, but are not lawfully acceptable proof marks.

Much more information on proof and proof marks, both British and foreign, may be found in 'Notes on the Proof of Shotguns and Other Small Arms', a booklet available from either Proof House at 5s. 9d. post free. Personal enquiries may be addressed to the Proof Masters at: The Proof House, Banbury Street, Birmingham, 5; or The Gunmakers Company, 48 Commercial Road, London, E.1.

CHAMBERS AND CARTRIDGE LENGTHS

Shotgun chambers are usually $2''$, $2\frac{1}{2}''$, $2\frac{3}{4}''$ or $3''$. All Eley cartridge cartons state the chamber length for which the cartridges are intended. The description does not refer to the length of the cartridge itself.

$2''$ cartridges are not normally used in any chamber length longer than $2''$. $2\frac{1}{2}''$ cartridges can be used in $2\frac{1}{2}''$ or $2\frac{3}{4}''$ guns, but cartridges intended for $2\frac{3}{4}''$ chambers have higher pressures and should not be used in $2\frac{1}{2}''$ chambers. Cartridges intended for $3''$ chambers should not be used in shorter chambers.

THE CARTRIDGE

A cartridge is a cylinder of paper or plastic (polyethylene), fitted at one end with a metal head containing an ignition device (percussion cap) and sealed at the other end by one of two closure methods – crimp or rolled turnover. Inside the cartridge is a propellent powder and a charge of spherical pellets of lead alloy called "shot". In between the shot charge and the propellant are several thick discs called wads which act together as a piston propelled by the powder gases.

When the trigger of a gun is pressed, the firing pin strikes the centre of the percussion cap, causing the priming composition to ignite and send a flame into the powder. As the powder burns it is transformed into a gas which expands to many times the volume that the powder occupied. The tremendous pressure generated must be released and it escapes by forcing open the cartridge closure and propelling the shot and wads in front of it along the barrel at very high speed.

Shot pellets are graded according to certain sizes, each having a number. The smaller the shot, the higher the number.

The most popular sizes for game and pigeon shooting are 5, 6 and 7; for rabbits 5 or 6; for duck and hare 4 and 5; and for clay pigeons 7, 8 or 9.

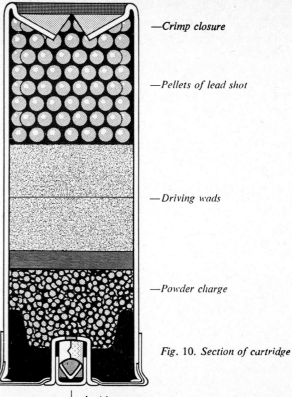

—Crimp closure

—Pellets of lead shot

—Driving wads

—Powder charge

Fig. 10. *Section of cartridge*

└—*Ignition system*

For clean kills, the pellets must have enough penetrating power and be sufficiently densely grouped to ensure that a vital spot is hit. Various brands of cartridges are available designed to meet the different conditions experienced in the field.

A good general purpose cartridge is the Eley Grand Prix which has $1\frac{1}{16}$ oz. shot and is suitable for most types of shooting at ranges up to about 45 yards.

Many people prefer a light load cartridge when they are shooting driven game; Impax is a good choice. Its 1 ounce load is perfectly adequate and gives less recoil resulting in more comfortable shooting over long periods.

At the other extreme, wildfowlers need *long* range, heavy load cartridges and one of the most popular choices is Alphamax. However, it is important to ensure that your gun is proof-marked for the higher pressures of these more powerful cartridges.

MAXIMUM RANGE

Maximum range is the greatest distance at which a gun will kill with certainty. It depends on two things:
(a) the density of the pattern formed by the shot;
(b) the striking energy of the individual pellets.

The heavier the shot, the greater its penetration power but as the size of the shot increases so the number of pellets in the load decreases.

It is instructive to fire at sheets of newspaper at different ranges and with various sizes of shot and so see the gun's pattern. Gunmakers do this on a metal plate and call the process "plating". To ensure that some pellets find a vital spot and make a clean kill it is reckoned that there should be about 130 pellets within a 30″ circle.

When carrying out this "plating" it must be noted that the shot should be fired at the plate or sheet of paper before the 30″ circle is drawn around the pattern. This is because it is impracticable to "sight" a shot gun with the accuracy of a rifle. A good even pattern with no "holes" in it is what the gunmaker looks for.

The following table shows the distance at which there are 130 pellets within a 30″ circle from a 12 bore gun firing standard cartridges loaded with shot sizes 4, 5, 6 and 7 through improved cylinder, half choke and full choke.

Shot sizes	No. 4	No. 5	No. 6	No. 7
Improved Cylinder ..	30 yd.	35	40	45
Half Choke	35 yd.	40	45	50
Full Choke	40 yd.	45	50	55

Target Area

As soon as the pellets leave the gun they start to spread, and the further they go the more they scatter. A large bird like a pheasant is remarkably small when plucked and when flying away from the shooter it offers a target little larger than a tennis ball. If the pellets scatter too widely all may miss the bird even though the gun is correctly pointed. Worse still, one or two may strike and only wound.

Pattern Density

The spread of shot from barrels of similar boring is the same irrespective of the calibre of the weapons. This means that as cartridges for the smaller bores contain lighter shot charges, the pattern density decreases for a given size of shot. In practice, the pattern density of each decreasing bore is the same at about three yards closer range: in other words, a 16 bore's range for 130 pellets in a 30 inch circle is about three yards less than a 12's; a 20 bore's about six yards less than a 12's, and so on. The number of pellets contained in the shot charges of standard load 2½ inch cartridges is given in Fig. 11a.

Striking Force

The striking energy of the pellets required for a clean kill depends on the size of the target. For instance, it is considered that small birds such as snipe should be hit with pellets having at least 0·5 ft. lb. energy, medium sized birds such as grouse require at least 0·85 ft. lb. energy for each pellet, and large birds such as geese require at least 1·5 ft. lb. energy for each pellet. Provided that the pattern density is sufficient for a given target, the killing range is therefore restricted by the pellet energy falling below that necessary for a particular target.

The striking energy in ft. lbs. of individual pellets at different distances for standard game cartridges is given in Fig. 11b.

Bore of Gun	No. 4 Shot	No. 5 Shot	No. 6 Shot	No. 7 Shot
12	181	234	287	361
16	159	206	253	319
20	138	179	219	276
28	96	124	152	191
·410	75	97	118	149

Fig. 11a. *Table showing the number of pellets and different sizes of cartridges.*

Size of Shot	Range in Yards					
	20	30	35	40	45	50
3	5·79	4·48	3·92	3·43	2·99	2·59
4	4·68	3·54	3·08	2·66	2·30	1·97
5	3·52	2·60	2·23	1·90	1·61	1·36
6	2·80	2·03	1·71	1·44	1·20	1·01
7	2·16	1·52	1·27	1·06	0·86	0·70

Fig. 11b. *Striking energy in ft. lbs. of individual pellets for standard game cartridges.*

Fig. 12. Safe ways of carrying a gun

SAFETY RULES

Shotgun design has evolved over 100 years to produce a weapon and cartridge which are basically safe. Nevertheless every year there are a number of shooting accidents

There are certain fundamental safety rules to be observed when handling a gun. Familiarity may cause them to be broken (unless they are so deeply ingrained as to be automatic), and then the inevitable accident happens.

The following rules should, therefore, be carefully observed and practised:

1. Never point a gun at anyone.
2. Always handle a gun as if it were loaded, even though you yourself have taken out the cartridges.
3. Carry it safely – either on the crook of the arm with the barrels pointing towards the ground, or on the shoulder with the triggers uppermost, pointing the barrels to the sky.
4. When taking the gun out of its case (and always while out shooting) look through the breech before loading to make sure there are no obstructions.
5. When loading, close the gun by bringing the stock upwards, not the barrels. This keeps the barrels pointing down at a safe angle throughout the operation.
6. When expecting a shot, walk with the gun pointing forward and towards the ground or up towards the sky, with the safety catch in the "safe" position. The safety catch locks the triggers.
7. Keep the safety catch at "safe" until the gun is being raised to the shoulder to fire.
8. Unload when negotiating any obstacle (even a low strand of wire or small ditch) or when putting the gun down.
9. Check that any gun is unloaded before taking it into a house, putting it into a vehicle, laying it down or picking it up, and after taking it from someone else.

Fig. 13. Dangerous behaviour

SAFETY IN THE FIELD

There are four sources of danger:
1. A gun which goes off accidentally.
2. A shot fired at game which hits a companion or some person not in sight, either directly or from pellets that ricochet.
3. A shot fired as the quarry passes between the shooter and another gun or a beater. This is particularly likely to happen when game is being driven to a line of guns.
4. Loading with the wrong size cartridge. A 20-bore cartridge may drop right into a 12-bore barrel, giving the appearance of an unloaded gun: if a cartridge of the correct size is then inserted, a burst barrel and a serious accident could result. A variation on this is a barrel blockage caused by mud or snow.

These can be avoided:
1. By following the Safety Rules on page 13.
2. By rough-shooting guns staying level with each other when walking, particularly when on either side of a hedge, and by never firing at a dangerous angle.
3. By the shooter always keeping in mind his "safety zones" when walking in line with other guns or taking part in a drive.
4. By keeping cartridges of different sizes separate, and checking that barrels are clear of mud and snow.

The safety zones are the areas within which the gun may be fired safely. If the quarry passes from one safety zone to another, the barrels must be lowered to point at the ground or raised by dropping the butt.

Fig. 14. *A dangerous swing – watch your safety zone*

Fig. 15. *Don't fire where you cannot see*

Finally, a gun must never be fired where the shooter cannot see; courting couples, farm workers having a break, and even berry-picking toddlers can turn up in most unlikely places!

FIELD LORE & COURTESY

The sportsman with a shotgun must not only learn how to handle a gun safely and efficiently, but also know some "field lore" – that is, something of the habits of the birds and animals he hunts and the best ways of getting within range of them. Anything that is wounded must be followed up at once and instantly dispatched, whatever the temptation to do something else. The shooting man must avoid damage to crops and treat valuable livestock and property with care. All this seems obvious, but it is very often forgotten.

The man who goes shooting is the guest of the people who live in the neighbourhood and he must behave as a guest, never taking or shooting anything to which he has no right. He must avoid damaging fences, and the trouble caused by such thoughtlessness as leaving a gate open.

If he takes shots beyond his weapon's maximum range he will cause suffering to the quarry he seeks by wounding instead of killing it. Never for a moment must he forget that his gun is a lethal weapon and can kill or maim at distances far in excess of the effective range for killing game and vermin etc.

WHAT TO SHOOT

Pigeons and rabbits have always been the mainstay of the rough shooter's sport. Rabbits are less common than in the days before the myxomatosis plague struck in 1954, but they still appear sporadically in places. Permission for shooting is usually more easily obtained than for game and in some cases the shooting rights may be rented.

The exclusive right to kill game on a landowner's property belongs to him; so long as he has not parted with his rights. There is almost no "free shooting" in England today. The owner of the land must give his permission or agree to let the shooting rights.

Woodpigeons are an agricultural pest and give challenging sport to the shooting man. They can be flighted at their roosting places or attracted by decoys set up on their favourite feeding grounds, while the shooter conceals himself in a hide.

Rabbits can be stalked when they are feeding, ferreted, stunk out or hunted out of marsh cover with a dog.

The shooting of game and wildfowl falls more to the lot of the experienced shooter.

The common method of obtaining the right to shoot on someone's land is to contact an owner-farmer and rent his shooting. It may be possible to obtain permission to shoot rabbits or pigeons free of charge at certain times. This is often a matter of being known to the farmer as a safe and reliable person but do not expect every farmer to greet you with open arms. Too many have had the experience of gun-happy 'cowboys' who would shoot a prize turkey as readily as a woodpigeon.

The right to shoot game is much more difficult and expensive to obtain. Owner-farmers may be contacted by advertising for a "rough shoot" in a local paper or in the *Shooting Times*, and country hotels in certain areas sometimes have shooting for their guests.

Hares: Strictly speaking there is no close season for hares on ordinary farmland, but they cannot be legally sold during the spring and summer (March to July inclusive) and are not usually shot during these months. Most organised hare shoots are held in January/February. On moorland and unenclosed areas, it is legal to shoot hares only from December 11th (July 1st in Scotland) to March 31st.

Deer: These are covered by separate legislation and in any case do not normally fall within the scope of the rough-shooter with a shotgun smaller than 12 bore or a rifle with a calibre below .240 in. Any cartridge shot size smaller than SSG is also illegal. There are close seasons for deer, but they may be controlled outside these seasons if damage can be proved.

Even on the coast there is virtually no free shooting today. Most of the foreshore in England is now controlled by wildfowling clubs which will require you to be a member before being allowed to shoot. This does not apply in Scotland, however, where access to the foreshore for shooting is a right except on Nature Reserves and so on. The local club in England can normally be contacted through The Wildfowlers Association of Great Britain and Ireland, 104 Watergate Street, Chester.

LEGAL REQUIREMENTS

You must comply with several legal requirements before you can go out shooting:

a) Section 2 of the Firearms Act which came into force on 1st August, 1968, regulates the system of shot gun certificates and restrictions on the possession, purchase and acquisition of shot guns.

The procedure for obtaining a certificate is as follows:
1. If you wish to have in your possession, or purchase or acquire a shot gun, you must obtain a shot gun certificate from your local Chief of Police. It is an offence not to do so unless you are in one of the categories in paragraph 3.

2. A shot gun is defined as "a smooth bore gun having a barrel not less than 24 inches in length, not being an air gun". Shot guns with barrels less than 24 inches in length are already subject to control under the Firearms Acts, 1937 and 1965, and you must apply to the police for a firearms certificate in order to acquire or possess them.

3. You do not need a shot gun certificate—
   i) if you are on a short visit to Great Britain. (If you stay in Great Britain for a total of more than 30 days in 12 months you must have a certificate.)
   ii) if you use someone else's shot gun on artificial targets at a place and time approved by the local chief officer of police.
   iii) if you borrow a shot gun from the occupier of private premises (including private land) and use it thereon in his presence.
   iv) if you are exempt from holding a firearm certificate under Part I of the Firearm Act, 1937 (if in doubt, consult the police).

4. You should obtain an application form from the police, from your gunsmith or from any shooting organisation or society to which you belong. When you have completed the form you must get it countersigned in the way described on the form. Unless the police tell you otherwise, you should take the completed form, with the fee, to your local police station.

5. You will be given a receipt by the police when you lodge your application, and if it is granted your certificate will be sent to you later: it may be some time before you receive it.

6. Holders of Certificates would be well advised to apply for their renewal in good time as the police are under no obligation to remind you that renewal is due. Once a Certificate has lapsed and if you still

have a shotgun in your possession, you are breaking the law.

7. There was a nominal fee of five shillings for initial certificates issued before November 1st 1968. The fee for certificates to be issued after 1st January 1969 are as follows:

	£	p
For a firearm certificate grant	2	50
For a firearm renewal and replacement.. ..	1	25
For a variation increasing the number of firearms	1	25
For a shotgun certificate grant or renewal ..		75
For a shotgun certificate replacement		37½

b) You must have a game licence to shoot any of the birds listed as game in the shooting list and also for Snipe, Jack Snipe, and Woodcock and in certain circumstances rabbits.

c) The shooting rights over land belong to the owner-occupier, that is *prima facie* the landlord. If an owner of land ceases to occupy his land, as for example when he leases it to a tenant, then the shooting rights over the leased land will pass to the tenant unless the landlord in the lease has specifically reserved those rights to himself or a third party. If the lease is silent as regards the shooting rights they pass to the tenant who is the occupier during the term of the lease. That is the law in England and Wales.

In Scotland it is exactly otherwise. There the shooting rights remain vested in the landowner unless he has specifically conveyed them to his tenant; if the lease is silent they remain with the landowner.

Tenant farmers under the Ground Game Act 1880 have an inalienable right to kill ground game (hares and rabbits) on the land in their occupation even if the shooting rights are reserved. But only the farmer himself and one other person duly authorised in writing by him may use firearms to do so, but even then not at night.

d) Certain birds and animals can be killed only during particular seasons of the year. These seasons are laid down by Act of Parliament as regards game in the Game Act 1911 and as regards wildfowl in the Protection of Birds Act 1954.

e) There are certain rules concerning those under 17 years of age. For details consult a gunmaker.

SHOOTING LIST

The following is a list of birds which can be legally shot. It is essential to know and recognise these as shooting a protected bird can lead to prosecution. Definitions of "game" vary according to various Acts of Parliament but the birds on the first list below may not legally be shot on Sundays or Christmas Day; but rabbits may. Wildfowl may be shot on Christmas Day and Sundays unless there is a County prohibition.

It is an offence to shoot any other wild bird. The protection of wild birds is governed by the Protection of Birds Act 1954. Changes may be made from time to time and if in doubt enquiries should be made at the local police station.

GAME (*Protected by the Game Act* 1831)

Pheasant	Grouse	Ptarmigan
Partridge	Blackgame	(in Scotland)
	*Hares	

*There are many exceptions as regards hares and rabbits in respect to game licences. Rabbits may be shot on Sundays and Christmas Day.

WILDFOWL

Waders

Snipe and Jacksnipe	Curlew (except	Moorhen
Godwit, Bar-tailed	Stone Curlew)	Whimbrel
Redshank, Common	Plover, Golden	Coot
	Plover, Grey	Woodcock

Geese

Bean	Greylag	Pink-footed
Canada		White-fronted

Ducks

Common Pochard	Long-tailed Duck	Shoveler
Scoter, Common	Mallard	Teal
Gadwall	Pintail	Tufted Duck
Garganey Teal	Scaup Duck	Velvet Scoter
Goldeneye		Wigeon

BIRDS WHICH MAY BE SHOT AT ANY TIME

Cormorant	Jay
Crow, Carrion	Magpie
Crow, Hooded	Red-breasted Merganser
Domestic Pigeon, gone feral	(in Scotland only)
Goosander (in Scotland only)	Rock-dove (in Scotland only)
Gull, Greater Blackbacked	Rook
Gull, Lesser Blackbacked	Shag
Gull. Herring	Starling
House Sparrow	Stock-dove
Jackdaw	Wood-pigeon

It is an offence to shoot any other wild bird.

Heavy fines can be incurred if certain birds and game are shot in the close season. The seasons given in the list below, therefore, must be strictly observed.

SHOOTING SEASONS (*All dates inclusive*)

Black Game	..	..	..	Aug.	20	—	Dec.	10
Grouse ..	..	..	..	Aug.	12	—	Dec.	10
Capercaillie	..	..	..	Oct	1	—	Jan.	31
Ptarmigan	..	..	..	Aug.	12	—	Dec.	10
Partridge	..	..	..	Sept.	1	—	Feb.	1
Pheasant	..	..	..	Oct.	1	—	Feb.	1
Snipe ..	..	..	..	Aug.	12	—	Jan.	31

Woodcock .. { Oct. 1 — Jan. 31 (*England and Wales*)
{ Sept. 1 — Jan. 31 (*Scotland*)

Wild duck } .. .. Sept. 1 — Jan. 31 (*Inland*)
Wild geese* } .. Sept. 1 — Feb. 20 (*on the Foreshore*)

*Other than Brent or Barnacle geese which are protected.

(*Note:* Foreshore is defined as "below high water mark of ordinary spring tides".)

Other Wild Birds   Sept. 1 — Jan. 31

Coot	Golden Plover
Curlew (not stone curlew)	Grey Plover
Bar-tailed Godwit	Common redshank
Moorhen	Whimbrel

HOW TO SHOOT

To be a good shot it is essential to have a gun that fits you and then you have to master three fundamental actions – gun mounting, stance and swing.

Fig. 17. Right eye in alignment with rib of gun.

Fig. 16. Stock in shoulder hollow, cheek pressed on stock

GUN MOUNTING

a) The gun should be firmly but not tightly held and the stock should nestle comfortably into the hollow between the collar bone and the shoulder bone.

b) Your head should be held upright and the stock should be brought up to the head and not vice versa.

c) Your cheek should be pressing sufficiently firmly along the comb of the stock so that the flesh is compressed.

d) Your right eye should then be in perfect alignment with the rib of the gun.

If you find it impossible to get into this position the gun probably does not fit you and needs altering.

It is best to keep both eyes open when using a shotgun, you can see the bird better and also judge distance and speed more accurately.

Having both eyes open introduces the problem of the "master eye". A right-handed shooter having a right "master eye" will have no difficulty in pointing the gun correctly. If the left eye is master, however, a right-handed shooter will be in difficulties for his gun will be actually pointing to the left of the object he is aiming at. Check which is your master eye as follows:

a) Extend your right arm and with your index finger point at some object with both eyes open.

b) Close your left eye and if your finger still points at the object your right eye is the master.

c) If your finger points some distance to the left of the object then the left eye is the master.

If you have a left master eye you have then three alternatives:

a) You can fire the gun from your left shoulder, but this is difficult for a right-hander.

b) A special "cross-over" stock can be fitted to the gun which compensates for this fault.

c) You will have to close, or partially close, the left eye.

Assuming the gun fits you, before even considering firing it, you should spend a considerable time practising gun mounting. Stand in front of a mirror with the gun in the ready position (see Fig. 19), push slightly forward with your left hand, and with your right hand raise the stock to your cheek and the butt into your shoulder.

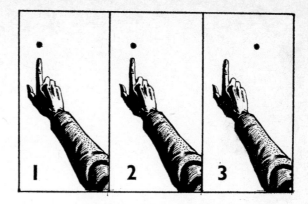

Fig. 18. *Using index finger to determine "master eye"*

1. *Both eyes open.*
2. *Left eye closed, right eye is master.*
3. *Left eye closed, left eye is master.*

Make sure that the butt of your gun travels in a direct line upwards; avoid thrusting forward and then drawing back. Practise this movement until you can bring your gun up in a smooth, swift action always making sure that it ends with your cheek tight on the stock and the right eye in the correct position. Practise this until you do it automatically.

STANCE

Stand with your feet comfortably spaced apart. Your body should be inclined forward sufficiently to bring your centre of balance onto the left or forward foot (but not in an exaggerated manner). Your left leg should be braced and your right heel just lifted clear of the ground. It should now be possible to swing the gun through a wide arc by rotating your body. Remember that the swing should come from pivoting your hips, for if the movement is made with your arms alone your head may well come off the stock – this is one of the commonest causes of missing.

Fig. 19. Correct position ready for action

Fig. 20. Correct position whilst firing

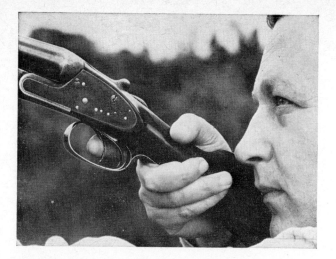

Fig. 21. Correct position of hand and trigger finger, although the right thumb could, with advantage, be further round the grip

For an incoming overhead shot, the gun is swung by bending your body backwards from the hips. Care should be taken to ensure that your cheek still remains firmly on the stock.

When out walking over rough ground it is obviously difficult to ensure a perfect stance every time, but it is always better to take your time and get the best stance possible rather than take a hurried, off-balance shot and almost certainly miss.

Fig. 22. Overhead shot. The left hand could have been reaching further up the barrel and the right thumb is a little too close to the top lever.

23

Fig. 23 *(left hand illustration) Incorrect position for overhead shot – off balance, cheek off stock and weight back on right foot*

Fig. 24 *(right hand illustration) A well-balanced position for overhead shot*

SWING AND LEAD

Probably the most fundamental fault in shooting is stopping the swing of the gun and deliberately aiming at the target. The secret of hitting a moving target is to keep the gun moving.

Start with the gun in the ready position and as soon as you see the bird, get the gun muzzles up on to it, moving with the target as you bring the butt of the gun smoothly into your shoulder. As you swing, move the muzzle ahead of the target (giving it a "lead"), press the trigger and continue swinging as your shot travels to the target.

Very briefly then the action broken down into detail is as follows (this is for a shot at a simple driven bird moving towards you and crossing from right to left which is the easiest for a right-handed person):

a) As soon as you see the target follow it with your eyes.

b) Pivot your body to the left, bringing the muzzle of your gun into alignment with the target (Fig. 25(1)).

c) As you swing with the target bring the gun into your shoulder and your cheek right on to the stock (Fig. 25(2)).

d) Still swinging, move the gun slightly ahead of the target, giving it a lead, and gently press the trigger

e) **Continue** your swing: do not stop to admire your handiwork.

Fig. 25. Aiming. (1) *Bring gun muzzle up in line with target.* (2) *Bring gun up to shoulder still aiming at target*

Broken down into sections like this shooting appears laboured and complicated, but if you practise to get all the actions correct and gradually speed them up you will have learnt the techniques which will shortly develop into swift, smooth, automatic reaction.

It is impossible to say how much "lead" you should give the target as this varies with angle and distance. What is certain, however, is that if the swing is stopped or jerked or an attempt made to intercept the bird by a direct aim, a miss will very likely result.

Between the moment of decision to fire, and the shot reaching a target 40 yards away there is a period of time made up as follows:

Interval	from	to	Time in secs.
Personal reaction time	Deciding to shoot	Pulling trigger	Average .275
Action Time	Pulling trigger	Striker hits cap	.005
Barrel Time	Striker hits cap	Shot leaves muzzle	
Flight Time	Shot leaves muzzle	Shot hits target	.135
			0.415

A bird flying at 40 m.p.h. at a range of 40 yards will have travelled over 32 feet during this time. This explains why it is essential that the gun is kept swinging, first to keep pace with the target and secondly to overtake the target so as to counteract the time lag involved.

Common reasons for missing include:

a) Lifting your head off the stock to look at the bird. This is particularly common on left to right crossing birds and high overhead birds.

b) Flinching just before firing.

c) Tilting the barrels of the gun to one side or the other.

d) Tilting your head down to the gun.

e) Swinging off balance and being unable to follow through.

f) Snatching at the trigger.

g) Aiming hopefully into a covey rather than selecting a bird as a target and shooting at that one.

h) Jerking the gun with the left hand rather than swinging smoothly.

One excellent method of becoming a proficient shot is to attend a shooting school or clay pigeon club which provides expert training in how to shoot (see page 29).

SHOOTING HINTS

GAME SHOOTING

The shooting of game is done in two main ways, either by walking up, sometimes over dogs, or by driving.

When either walking up or driving, shots should never be fired until the line has been properly formed. Guns should be unloaded between drives.

WALKING-UP

When walking up, two guns (or as many as five or six) walk steadily in line about 30 yards apart. If they are shooting partridges then their walking is planned to keep the coveys within the boundaries of the shoot and to manoeuvre them into thick cover where they will lie until the guns are well within range.

Usually nearly all the birds are going away from the shooter at varying angles and rising, perhaps quite sharply, and due allowance must be made for this by the angle of the swing, which must be upward as well as across.

To ensure safety, walking guns must keep exactly in line with each other (see Fig. 26). When a shot is fired, the whole line should stop until the shooter has reloaded and the bird has been gathered and then all move on together in line again. When any obstacle has to be negotiated, those who have crossed it first must wait until the last one is over and then the whole line goes forward once more.

Fig. 26. *A dangerous position – out of line*

DRIVING

When driving, the birds come forward to the guns, who are either concealed in butts or behind a hedge or standing in woodland rides. The butts screen the shooter from the front and are made to harmonise with their surroundings. Beaters about 40 yards apart, or less in close cover, form up in line a considerable distance from the butts and move towards them driving the partridges or grouse on the intervening land forward and over the guns. The same thing applies in driving pheasants, except that the beaters keep much closer together in the

27

thick cover of the woods or kale. Beware of "stops" at a shoot and other people who may be hidden behind hedgerows.

You can learn quite a lot about shooting by volunteering to help in beating and your services will be welcomed. It is great fun, good exercise and very instructive.

Where possible, driven birds should be shot as they are approaching. This means that the swing must be upwards and the barrels must blot out the bird before the trigger is pressed (see Fig. 24).

In shooting at birds that have passed the butts and are going away, the swing needs to be downwards.

A lone shooter must stalk his quarry as in the case of a rabbit out feeding, or wait where it will come within range, as in the case of a pigeon coming in to roost or to feed. It is possible for the lone gunner to manoeuvre partridges into thick cover such as roots or clover, but this is much more easily done with two or more companions.

WOODPIGEON SHOOTING

The woodpigeon is an agricultural pest in Britain and official estimates put the pigeon population at certain times as high as 10 million birds, which eat 500 tons of food each day. Woodpigeons provide good sport at low cost with a real challenge for those who are interested

in field craft: it is not difficult to shoot half a dozen pigeons, but the man who can shoot 100 is a master of several skills in addition to marksmanship.

Woodpigeon shooting takes place all the year round and the shooter will probably enjoy his sport alone. The pleasures are similar to those of wildfowling – the challenge of coming to terms with wary birds and the development of local knowledge which makes each woodpigeon shooting day completely different from all the others.

The main forms of the sport are decoying and flight shooting. When using decoys the shooter finds where the birds are feeding and sites himself on the spot concealed in the hide, after putting out a number of artificial decoys or dead pigeons on the feeding ground.

Flight shooting usually takes place in the later afternoon at the edge of woodland areas used by the birds as winter roosts.

Most shooting men think of decoying when they consider woodpigeon shooting and this is certainly the mainstay of the sport in the summer months but, in winter, time may be divided between decoys and flight shooting.

There is no need to regard woodpigeon decoying as "a poor man's sport" in any sense. There is no doubt that the sight of a woodpigeon in high, fast flight being turned as if by an invisible cord and lured into range over a pattern of decoys is one which equals any aspect of shooting and it has the added satisfaction that the shooter can be certain that it was all his own work.

Fig. 27. An informal clay pigeon shoot

CLAY PIGEON SHOOTING

This is one of the most popular forms of shotgun shooting today as it is a satisfying sport in itself and also forms excellent practice for all forms of game shooting. The best clay pigeon shots are amongst the **most skilled shooters in the world at any type of target.**

The targets are $4\frac{1}{4}''$ diameter saucers of baked pitch and chalk which are thrown from a mechanical catapult called a trap. Their shape, together with the spin imparted by the throwing arm, produces a steady soaring flight. Clay pigeons hurtle from the traps at over 40 m.p.h. and it is very satisfying to see them disappear into puffs of dust when you are on target.

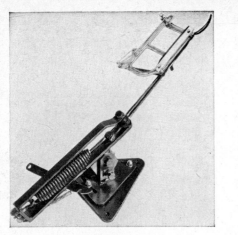

Fig. 28. *Clay pigeon trap*

shooter is ready to fire (gun at the shoulder) he calls "Pull" and the trap operator releases the bird. Each shooter moves along the line, thereby taking birds at five different angles. Down-the-line is probably the easiest layout to install and because of this is the most widely practised form of the sport.

A 'Skeet' installation consists of a semi-circle of 7 firing points with a high trap house at the left-hand side and a low trap house at the right. Targets are thrown on specified lines of flight and shooters move round the semi-circle from firing point to firing point so that they take shots at going away, crossing and driven birds. Single targets from each trap house are taken at each station followed by doubles (i.e., a bird from each trap house) thrown simultaneously, at five of the stations.

"Sporting clays" are thrown to simulate various shots taken when game shooting, such as high pheasants, driven grouse, crossing partridges, woodpigeon, springing teal, bolting rabbits and so on. Shooting schools generally concentrate on sporting clays because they are the finest practice for game shooting.

Clay pigeon shooting is lively, enjoyable, challenging and it combines the innate desire to try one's skill at hitting a moving target with the satisfaction of handling a gun, the social atmosphere of a club and the opportunity to shoot in friendly competition if you wish.

If you want to know more about it, talk to your local cartridge retailer or write to The Clay Pigeon Shooting Association, Angel Road, London, N.18.

There are over 400 gun clubs in the country, most being affiliated to the Clay Pigeon Shooting Association which organises the competitive aspect of the sport. Most clubs are keen to have new members and experienced shooters are often willing to help novices with some coaching.

Clay pigeon shooting is surprisingly varied. There are three main types, Down-the-line, Skeet and Sporting. Many clubs can offer two of these and some all three.

In "Down-the-line", each of 5 guns fires in turn at targets thrown as going away birds. The trap is sited 16 yards in front of the line of competitors. When the

GUN CLEANING

A good shotgun will deteriorate very little in a lifetime if given proper care and if examined and overhauled occasionally by a gunsmith. Gun cleaning has become much simpler since the introduction of the non-corrosive cartridge, but is still necessary especially if the gun has been used in wet conditions.

A cleaning outfit is essential and should consist of a cleaning rod, pieces of newspaper about 6″ square, flannelette patches, a bristle or phosphor-bronze brush, a wool mop and a can of gun cleaning oil.

First remove any visible residue in the barrels by pushing through a piece of newspaper rolled into a ball and then wipe out the bore with a dry patch. Should there be any lead deposit, remove it with the brush, using a little turpentine if necessary; never use a steel brush, particularly of the turk's head variety, as this will damage the barrel.

Next, using another patch, wipe through the barrels again and finally apply a coating of oil with the wool mop. Using a feather clean round and under the extractors with the quill end.

Sparingly apply a thin lubricating oil with the feather end to the extractors, the triggers and the base of the ribs. A little linseed oil should be well rubbed into the stock and the metalwork of the gun wiped over with a cloth impregnated with thin oil.

If the gun has become very wet or has been used under extremely cold conditions, examine it again the next day

Fig. 29. Cleaning equipment

1. *Scrub out barrel and loosen fouling with a phosphor bronze wire brush wetted with cleaner, until discolouration disappears.*

2. *Dry out with several patches until clean.*

3. *Apply cleaner generously on a soft bristle brush or Wool mop.*

to see if there is any sweating, and if necessary carry out the cleaning procedure again.

CLOTHING

Whilst this is largely a matter of individual taste, there are certain essentials. All garments should be comfortable and harmonize with the surroundings. The coat should be loose enough to ensure easy movement when worn over thick woollies. There is nothing more miserable than to be cold when shooting, and warmth needs to come from the coat itself and the clothing worn under it. Shooting in a mackintosh or overcoat is difficult, and in bad weather a loose smock such as paratroopers wear is very practical.

Breeches are the best nether garments from every point of view. When thick cover with brambles are to be encountered, leggings give good protection. Although plusfours are popular they have considerable disadvantages.
For walking, boots with nails are preferable to rubber boots.

Any colour that makes the shooter conspicuous against his background should be avoided. A hat or cap will partially conceal the whiteness of the face. In cold weather the hands present a problem. Some shooters like to wear mittens. An alternative is to cut the forefinger off a pair of knitted woollen gloves, and thus leave the trigger-finger free.

It is perfectly safe to carry cartridges in the coat pockets. On a really wet day, however, unless you are using waterproof cartridges, the cases may get damp and swell so that they will not fit in the gun. On such occasions it is better to transfer them to trouser pockets.

Fig. 30. Example of suitable clothing

A "poacher's-pocket" with waterproof lining inside the coat is useful to the lone gunner for carrying the bag, but a haversack is often more comfortable.

GUN DOGS

A dog is a great asset to the shooting man, particularly the solitary rough-shooter. Handling a dog in the field gives as much pleasure in many cases as the shooting itself. For these reasons it is usually worth while to buy a dog for the purpose. A retriever such as a Labrador will be invaluable for fetching shot birds from inaccessible places and picking up crippled birds which might otherwise escape. It may also be taught to flush birds from patches of cover.

Spaniels can be taught to hunt through cover and retrieve and they also make good companions and house dogs. Labradors are the commonest single breed used for shooting today and the working strains make excellent dual purpose animals. A weaned puppy will cost from £10 upwards according to its breeding. Do not start training too early. The first lessons in obedience to whistle and to commands such as "sit" can begin when the puppy is 3–4 months old.

Retrieve training should not be attempted before 6 months. Even without training many puppies will carry a stick or a slipper before 6 months and when this happens the young dog should be encouraged to bring it to the hand, the object then being very gently removed from his grip. This must not be allowed to degenerate into a tug-of-war.

All training should be a happy game for a young dog with his master in full control. One perfectly performed lesson is of more value than six attempts which are only partly successful. All orders should be within the dog's

Fig. 31. *Gun-dog retrieving*

capability and must be enforced: never go on with a lesson if the dog becomes bored.

Retrieving of game can be attempted at about one year old. If this is done very much earlier the animal may possibly become "hard-mouthed", damaging birds while retrieving.

There are many excellent books on dog training and you should not be deterred from trying to break a dog because you have never done it before. Dog handling is an important and fascinating aspect of shooting and for many people it helps to give enormous pleasure even where game is not plentiful.

Conclusion

Shooting is a fascinating sport which has both practical application and pure enjoyment value. To get the most out of it, you must be prepared to learn to shoot well, to shoot safely and to act responsibly.

Game Licences (obtainable at most Post Offices)

One year, expiring July 31	£6
1st August – 31st October	£4
1st November – 31st July	£4
Any continuous period of 14 days	£2

A few useful books

Know Your Law	price 20p
Rabbiting and Ferreting	price 25p
Predatory Birds in Britain	price 40p
Predatory Mammals in Britain	price 40p
Stalking..	price 25p

all post free from

**The British Field Sports Society
26 Caxton Street, London SW1H 0RG**

THE SIX GOLDEN RULES

The following rules must be strictly observed when handling a gun. They are reproduced from the *Gun Code*, published by the British Field Sports Society in conjunction with The Wildfowlers' Association of Great Britain and Ireland.

BREAK ONE OF THESE RULES AND DEATH OR SERIOUS INJURY MAY FOLLOW FOR A FRIEND OR A STRANGER, FOR A MEMBER OF YOUR FAMILY OR FOR YOU.

1 **Never point your gun at any person.**

2 **Never carry your gun in a way that it can point at any person.**

3 **Never swing your gun across the line between yourself and another person.**

4 **Never shoot where you cannot see.**

5 **Never cross an obstacle without first unloading your gun.**

6 **Never leave your gun loaded.**

Check when taking it out.

Check before handing it to any person.

Check before laying it down.

Check before entering a vehicle.

Check before taking it into your home.

Check before putting it away.

Printed in Great Britain by Terry & Nephew Ltd., Dewsbury